Reading W
Everyday W

LEVEL 5

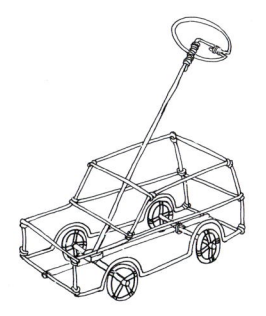

Wire is wonderful

Dawn Ridgway

Series Editor – Jean Conteh

MACMILLAN

About this Book

To the Teacher or Parent

This is a story about a child who faces problems after his parents die. It shows us how we can often overcome our problems if other people help us, and how important our families are to us.

Both boys and girls will enjoy this story, and learn a lot from it. The simple language and the pictures will help them to understand it. The story is divided into four chapters, as follows:

Chapter	page
1 A lucky find	3
2 Plans	13
3 Good news and bad news	25
4 What happens next?	35

The book is designed for children to read on their own. Use it like this:

- Before you give the book to the children, see if they can read the title. Ask them to look at the picture on the cover and tell you what they think the story will be about.
- Ask the children if they have seen anything made of wire, such as toys. If possible, show the children some wire toys, so they can talk about them.
- Talk about the problems children have if no one can support them – such as finding food, going to school and so on.
- Let the children read the book by themselves, asking for help if they need it. Afterwards, ask if they enjoyed it.
- Let the children look at pages 39 and 40, where there are questions and activities to help them understand and enjoy the story better.

Above all, let the children enjoy reading the book. This will make them interested in reading. They will want to learn to read for themselves, and become independent readers.

Chapter 1

A lucky find

Kabo used a stout stick to poke around in the smelly rubbish heap.

The day was hot. The stink of the rotting rubbish and the noise of the flies buzzing round it made Kabo feel sick.

Kabo was thirteen years old. He had worked on the dump for the last year, ever since his parents had died when their house caught fire. He did not know what else to do. His grandparents lived far away, and he did not know how to find them.

Suddenly, Kabo's stick hit something hard. He pushed aside a pile of rotting vegetables, and there was a large coil of wire! Kabo pulled as hard as he could. There was a second coil underneath it. The wire was covered in dirt and rubbish, but it was not rusty. In fact, it looked new.

Kabo was amazed. The dustbin men usually took anything valuable before they dumped the rubbish on the heap.

Kabo cleaned the dirt off the wire as well as he could. He worked quickly, as he did not want anyone else to see him. Otherwise, they would want some of the wire. Worse still, they might steal it all from him. He did not have anything better to clean the wire with than old leaves and pieces of newspaper from the rubbish heap. But, as he cleaned it, he felt how strong the wire was.

When he had cleaned the wire as well as he could, Kabo put it in the old, rusty supermarket trolley he used to carry his things in. He covered the wire with some old newspapers he had found on the heap that morning.

He pushed the trolley over the stones and mud at the side of the rubbish heap. It felt very heavy. His arms and back ached. The trolley bumped over the rough ground.

Luckily, none of the other rubbish pickers looked up as Kabo and his trolley rattled past.

7

Kabo pushed the heavy, wobbling trolley down the rough road. He walked as quickly as he could along the row of shacks where the rubbish pickers lived.

There were only a few children and a couple of dogs to watch him as he hurried past. All the adults were away, working to make money so they could feed their children.

At last, Kabo reached the tiny shack where he had lived since his parents died. He had built it himself with wood that he had found on the rubbish heap, and corrugated iron left from his parents' house after the fire. He lifted the piece of wood that he used for a door, took the wire from the trolley and carried it inside the shack.

Kabo put the wood back over the doorway of his shack and sat on the mud floor beside the wire.

There were very few things inside the shack. There was just a box with a blanket, a few clothes, an old plate Kabo had found on the rubbish heap and some bottles. There was a wooden frame Kabo had made with sticks and string. That was where he slept.

The wire lay in the middle of the shack. It filled a lot of the space. It was the most precious thing there. Kabo felt very happy that he had found it.

But he was also very worried that someone would try to steal it from him. It was at times like this that he missed his parents most.

He wished he could find his grandparents. He wished there was someone to help him, but the fire had left him with nobody.

Suddenly, there was a loud knock. Kabo jumped up in alarm.

'It's only me!' said a loud, friendly voice. Kabo hurried to move the piece of wood from the entrance to the shack. His friend, Sandile, was standing outside. Kabo grabbed him quickly, and pulled him into the shack.

Sandile was surprised.

'What's going on?' he asked.

'I've found something at the rubbish heap,' said Kabo. 'And it's worth a lot of money.'

Chapter 2

Plans

Kabo and Sandile sat together in the shack for a long time. They talked about what they could do with the wire.

Kabo wanted to find a way of selling it to someone honest, who would pay him a fair price for it.

'Why do you want to sell the wire?' asked Sandile. 'You could make things with it. Then you could sell them. You could make more money than if you just sold the wire as it is now.'

Kabo thought about this for a while.

'Yes,' he said. 'You're right! If I made things and sold them, I could buy more wire and make more things. I would have money to buy food, and maybe...'

He stopped. He looked as if he might cry.

'Maybe what?' asked Sandile. He was surprised that Kabo was sad. He should feel happy to have the wire.

'Maybe I could find a way to go to my grandparents,' said Kabo.

'Do you know where they live?' asked Sandile. He was surprised. Kabo had never mentioned his grandparents before.

'No,' said Kabo, sadly. 'We used to go in a bus to see them, but I don't know the name of the place. They sent letters to my parents, but they all got burned in the fire.'

The boys sat in silence in the dark shack. Sandile wondered what it was like to have no parents or grandparents. He felt sorry for Kabo. Then he had an idea.

'Come on!' he said. 'Let's go and ask my dad to help us learn how to make things with the wire. I think my mum is cooking, as well.'

Kabo looked at his friend and smiled. Sandile and his parents were kind to him, but Kabo knew they did not have much money.

Together, the boys loaded the wire back into the trolley.

Kabo and Sandile pushed the trolley down the track that led from the rubbish heap and the shacks to the place where Sandile lived. Sandile's family lived in a small house. His father, Mr Pule, had a small workshop next to the house.

Sandile's father was a mechanic. He fixed cars to make money. He did not have many tools, so he could only make small repairs. But he tried his best and did not charge high prices, like the big garage on the main road to the city. So people brought their cars and broken metal things to him, instead of going there.

Mr Pule was in his workshop when he heard the trolley rattling on the rough ground. He looked round and saw the boys pushing the heavy trolley with the two coils of wire inside.

'What's that you've got, boys?' he called out.

'It's some wire I found on the rubbish heap, Mr Pule,' replied Kabo. 'We've come to ask if you can help us learn to make things with it.'

'Well,' said Mr Pule, smiling, 'bring it in here and let's have a look at it.'

Eagerly, the boys pushed the trolley into the workshop and lifted the coils of wire onto the workbench.

'It's very good wire,' said Mr Pule. He bent and twisted it in his hand. It was thick, but bendy.

'I will need to cut it for you with my big wire-cutters. Then you can use the pliers to bend it into the shapes you want.'

The boys looked at each other. They were excited. They would be able to make all kinds of things with the wonderful wire.

'Can you show us how to make things, Dad?' asked Sandile.

19

Mr Pule smiled at the boys. Just then, Sandile's mother came to the doorway of the workshop.

'Hello, Kabo,' she said. 'How are you today?'

She felt sorry for Kabo, and tried her best to help him. But there was never enough money to go round. As well as Sandile, she had two other children.

She worried about Kabo. She had never talked to him about the fire, but she sometimes wondered if she should.

But she could not talk to Kabo now. Sandile was excited about the wire. He wanted to tell his mother the plans they had for it.

'That's great,' said Mrs Pule, when he finished explaining it all to her. 'Now, come inside and wash your hands. It's time to eat.'

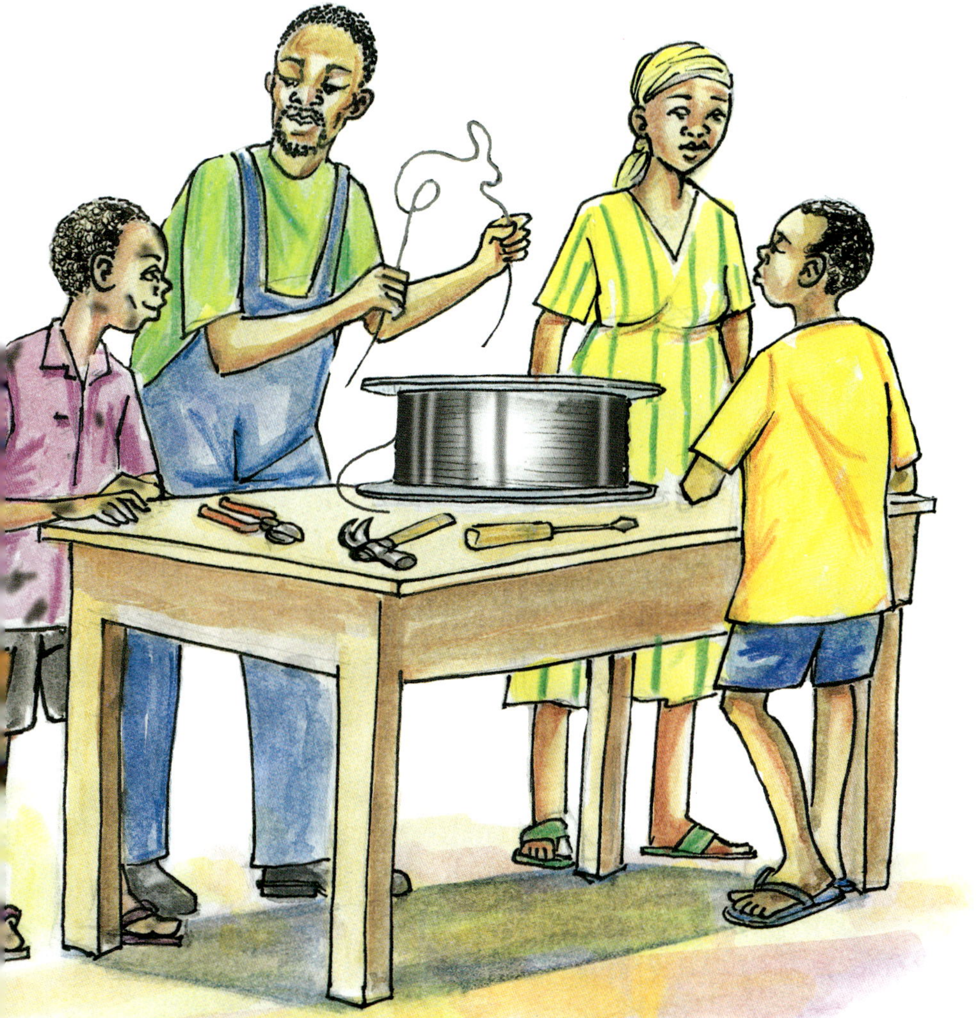

Kabo was glad he could eat with Sandile's family. Usually, he just tried to cook a few potatoes and whatever else he could find. He used one of the big fires that were always burning by the rubbish heaps.

He was always hungry. The food Sandile's mother cooked smelled delicious.

He tried not to show how hungry he was. He knew that there was not a lot of food for the whole family, and that everyone else was hungry too. They all sat together and shared what they had.

While they were eating, Mrs Pule noticed how sad Kabo looked, even though he had been so happy about the wire. She decided that, after the meal, she would talk to him. And that is what she did.

'Kabo,' she called quietly when the meal was finished. 'Come here. I want to talk to you.'

Kabo and Mrs Pule talked for a long time. When Kabo told her how his grandparents' letters had been burnt in the fire, tears rolled down his cheeks.

He wished he had a family, like Sandile, but he had nobody. Sandile and his parents were kind to him, but he always went back to his dark shack to sleep alone.

When Kabo left that evening, Mrs Pule thought about everything he had said to her. She knew she had to help him find his grandparents. She must find a way to let his grandparents know that Kabo was all alone and needed their help. She began to make her plans.

Chapter 3

Good news and bad news

Mr Pule let the boys keep the wire in his workshop. Kabo was pleased. He thought nobody would try to steal it from there.

A few days later, it was a school holiday. Sandile came to Kabo's shack to call him to the workshop.

'Dad says he will show us how to make things with the wire today,' he said. 'He says we can work at the bench while he repairs a car.'

'Great!' Kabo said. 'We can make lots of things! Toy cars! Toy bicycles! Toy windmills! Toy aeroplanes!'

The boys worked very hard that day.

Mr Pule lent them pliers and wire-cutters, and showed them how to use these tools.

It was hard work. The wire scratched the boys' fingers and made them bleed. They wanted to give up. But Mr Pule would not let them.

'Look at my hands,' he said. 'They get scratched when I mend cars. But I don't give up.'

At the end of the day, they had made a lot of things. Some of them were not very good. They felt a little disappointed. But Mrs Pule admired all the things they had made, and said they should go into town the next day to try to sell them.

'Now,' she said. 'Come into the house to eat. Then, I want to talk to you, Kabo.'

After supper, Kabo and Mrs Pule sat together at the table while the other children cleared up.

'Listen, Kabo,' said Mrs Pule. 'I've been thinking about how to find your grandparents. I went to the newspaper office yesterday, and told them your story.'

Kabo looked up at her. He felt worried that if people knew what had happened to him, maybe the police would try to arrest him. Mrs Pule saw that he was worried. She smiled and went on speaking.

'No,' she said. 'Don't feel worried. The people who work for the newspaper want to help. They say they will print your photo and your name. Then perhaps someone will see it who knows your grandparents. They say we should go to the newspaper office and talk to the editor.'

The next day was Saturday. Mr Pule helped the boys carry all the wire things they had made into town in his car.

They found an open space near the railway station and the bus station. Mr Pule helped Sandile and Kabo set all the wire things out for everyone to see. Then he left them and went home.

Kabo and Sandile sat with their wire toys all day.

At first, nobody looked at the toys. Then, a man picked up a wire car.

'This is a good car,' he said. 'I'll buy it for my son. How much is it?'

Kabo and Sandile looked at each other. This was their first sale! The man paid them what they asked, and went off with the car.

After that, more people stopped and looked at their wire toys. They did not all buy, but they were very interested in the toys. They asked the boys how they had made them. Some people asked if they had more toys, or if they had different kinds.

When Mr Pule came for them at the end of the day, they had not sold many toys, but they felt happy that many people were interested in them.

The next day, Kabo and Sandile went back to the space by the railway station. This time, more people bought the wire toys from them. By the end of the day, they had sold most of the toys. Some people asked if they would bring more the next weekend.

By the end of the day, they were tired, but full of excitement. As Mr Pule drove them home, they talked about all the toys they could make with the wonderful wire from the rubbish heap.

Kabo did not go to school because there was nobody to pay his fees. So he worked on the toys while Sandile was at school. Sandile helped as much as he could.

At weekends, they took the wire toys to the space by the railway station to sell them. They kept as much money as they needed to buy more wire, and Kabo had some to buy things he needed to make his shack more comfortable. Mr Pule let them keep the wire and the toys in his workshop.

One day, Mrs Pule took Kabo to the newspaper office. The editor listened to his story. He took Kabo's photo, and promised that he would print the story in the next day's paper. This is the article he wrote:

Do you know this boy?

Kabo Mwanga is thirteen years old. His parents died in a fire last year. Since then, Kabo has been living alone. His grandparents live in a rural area. We are trying to find them. If you think you know who Kabo's grandparents are, please get in touch with the newspaper.

When Kabo saw the article, he felt excited. Perhaps his grandparents would see it, and come to find him. But he also felt worried.

What if the police took him away because he did not go to school and lived in the shacks by the rubbish heaps?

For the next few days, he made more wire toys and thought about his grandparents.

On Saturday, Kabo and Sandile went to sell the toys in town. Their toys were very popular now. They were busy all day. But Kabo noticed a man who stood nearby for a long time and watched him. The man was young. He did not say anything. Later, when Kabo looked for him again, he had gone.

A few days later, Kabo was working in Mr Pule's workshop. He was thinking about the toys he was making. He was trying hard to make the wire bend into a good circle. He did not hear Mrs Pule come into the workshop. When she spoke, he looked up in surprise.

'Kabo,' she said softly. 'Come into the house. I'm sorry, but there is some bad news. The newspaper editor has come to talk to you. I'm afraid your grandparents are dead.'

Chapter 4

What happens next?

Kabo felt very sad when he heard about his grandparents. He did not want to make any more wire toys. He wanted to stay in his shack all day by himself. Sandile felt sorry for him. But he felt angry with him at the same time. If Kabo did not make wire toys, they would not have enough to sell.

So, even though he did not want to, Kabo tried to make the toys. But it was hard. What was he going to do, without any family to help him?

Two weeks later, Kabo and Sandile were together at their wire toy stall. Kabo saw the young man they had seen before. He stood for a long time beside the stall, watching the boys.

When the young man left, Kabo felt very scared.

'Did you see that man?' he asked Sandile. 'I think he's a policeman, and he wants to arrest me.'

'No, I don't think so,' Sandile said. He tried to make Kabo feel better. 'Just forget about him.'

But Kabo felt so scared that he did not want to go to the market again. The next day, he stayed in the workshop to make more toys. Sandile went alone. The young man came again. This time, he talked to Sandile. They talked for a long time.

When Sandile went home that evening, he called to Kabo.

'Come here, Kabo,' he said. 'There is someone who wants to meet you.'

Kabo came out of the workshop. He stopped and stared. Standing beside Sandile was the young man!

Kabo was just about to speak when Sandile said, 'Kabo, this is your uncle. His name is Thebe. He saw your photo in the newspaper. He's your father's younger brother. But he quarrelled with your father a long time ago. He has stayed alone since then.'

Kabo and his Uncle Thebe looked at each other for a while, and then shook hands.

The next day, Kabo went with his uncle to the room where he stayed. It was very small. Thebe did not have a job, and was very poor, but he was very friendly.

Kabo began to feel comfortable with him. He thought he looked a little like his father.

Kabo and Thebe visited each other many times in the next few weeks. Slowly, they got to know each other.

One day, Kabo said, 'Uncle Thebe, do you want to help us make wire toys? You can help us to sell them, and we will try to make more money.'

Thebe looked at his nephew.

'What a good idea!,' he said. 'And I've got an idea, too. Do you want to come and live with me? My room is not very big, but it's better than your shack by the rubbish heaps.'

Kabo suddenly felt very happy. He had a family at last. He knew that the future would not be easy, but maybe, together, he and his uncle would be all right.

1 Have you seen any wire toys, like the ones Kabo and Sandile made? Do people make them in your home town or village? Find out if they do, and then try to find out how they are made. Here are some photos of wire toys from different parts of Africa. Look in an atlas for the countries mentioned here.

A toy in Cameroon

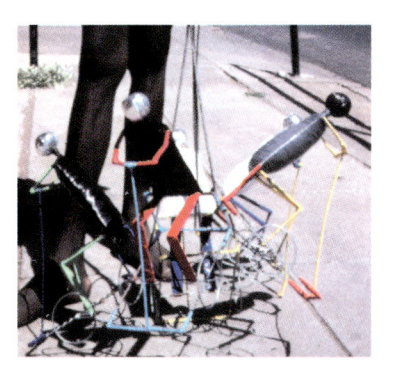

A toy in Botswana

Toys in Zimbabwe

A toy in Mozambique

Activity page

39

Activity page

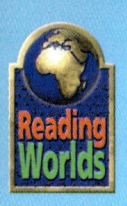

2 Have you seen anyone making wire toys? Do you have any of your own – or have you tried making them? Try drawing some pictures of different kinds of wire toys you might like to make.

3 Imagine you are Kabo. How do you think he felt after the fire, when his parents died? Write a few sentences about how he felt and what he did.

4 Read the first chapter of the story again. Make a list of all the words and phrases that tell you that Kabo was scared of the other rubbish pickers. Why do you think Kabo felt scared?